DRAMA FOR

Pocketbook

By Brian Radcliffe

Published by:

Teachers' Pocketbooks
Laurel House, Station Approach,
Alresford, Hampshire SO24 9JH, UK
Tel: +44 (0)1962 735573
Fax: +44 (0)1962 733637
E-mail: sales@teacherspocketbooks.co.uk
Website: www.teacherspocketbooks.co.uk

*Teachers' Pocketbooks is an imprint of
Management Pocketbooks Ltd.*

Series Consultant: **Brin Best**.

© Brian Radcliffe 2007.

This edition published 2007.

ISBN 978 1 903776 77 3

British Library Cataloguing-in-Publication
Data – A catalogue record for this book is
available from the British Library.

Design, typesetting and graphics by Efex Ltd.
Printed in UK.

Contents

Introduction

On my first day teaching at my present school I was introduced at staff briefing as 'the new drama supply teacher'. The response to this announcement was a loud and prolonged burst of applause, accompanied by cries of 'What a relief!' and 'Thank God!' I felt like the US Cavalry appearing over the hilltop to relieve the besieged wagon train. I wondered if I should renegotiate my terms of settlement immediately.

The reason for the enthusiastic welcome was that my arrival signalled the end of drama cover. In the absence of a dynamic and creative Head of Drama through illness, Physics, French, Technology and RE teachers had been sharing the load of covering the lessons. For some it had proved all too much:

'It always ends in a fight'
'I can't get them to hear me with all the noise'
'I like to keep them behind desks so I know where they are'

Drama has that effect on some teachers.

Introduction

So why should I suggest that those same teachers should not merely overcome initial trepidation, but be open to exploring the possibility that drama might actually enhance the quality of learning?

Primarily, it's because of what I believe as a teacher:

- The **quality of learning** is more important than the style of teaching (although one may have an effect on the other)
- Students come to their learning with a great deal to contribute, and we as teachers are **collaborators** with them in enhancing their learning
- The **direction** of learning should, where possible, be in the hands of the student
- While schemes of work and exam syllabuses might give destinations for that learning, the road we travel can be **flexible**
- Drama offers a series of techniques that **stimulate learning, promote collaborative endeavour** and give **a map** to follow for at least the next few miles

Introduction

Whether you teach in a primary or secondary school, and whether you come to this
book as confident or hesitant, enthusiastic or nervous it will:

- Show you how drama techniques address current
  understandings of how students learn
- Provide seven banks of drama techniques and
  explain the aspects of learning that they each
  enhance
- Offer more than 150 creative ideas for using these
  techniques in both a cross-curricular and single
  subject context
- Tackle issues of classroom management with clear,
  practical advice

Then you'll be ready to step into the spotlight.

Beginners, please.

Drama as Active Learning ◀

 Games

 Narrative

 Character

 Stylisation

 Analogies

 Dilemmas and Options

 Teacher in Role and Using Props

Drama as Active Learning

Flexing the muscles

There's a difference between the sports fan who experiences the thrill of the game from the comfort of an armchair and the one who participates: a different level of engagement, a different quality of involvement and a lasting benefit for the one who participates. It's the same for learning.

Drama encourages **participation in learning** since it is:

- Engaging and varied
- Brain-friendly
- Challenging
- Student-centred
- Collaborative
- Rewarding

Engaging and varied

A drama-based activity encourages involvement right from the start:

- Usually there's the opportunity to **get up and move**. Oxygenated blood pumps around the body and stimulates the brain.
- Everyone becomes a **performer**. However, as there's no audience, the extrovert has no need to demand attention and the introvert has less fear of observation
- **Perspectives** constantly **change** as the activity progresses
- The disaffected student is drawn in by **curiosity**
- The most gifted student is stimulated by the **infinite opportunity**

Brain-friendly

There are learning opportunities for a range of intelligences:

Linguistic – the writers and speakers

Logical-mathematical – the sequencers and classifiers

Visual-spatial – the picture creators

Musical – the rhythm and melody makers

Intrapersonal – the reflectors

Interpersonal – the group-makers

Bodily-kinaesthetic – the mime and model makers

Spiritual – the dreamers and seers

Naturalist – the environmentalists

When drama is used, it's **inclusive** of each student's personal mix of intelligences and the blend of intelligences in each group of students.

Brain-friendly

Neurologists have identified a variety of processing centres in the brain, often referred to in lateral terms for simplicity. Drama can bring all these into action:

Right
The big picture
Imagination
Music
Rhythm
Colour
Ideas

Left
Problem-solving
Sequencing
Detail
Logic
Analysis

Because it's both **cognitive** (uses logical understanding) and **affective** (uses emotion and feeling), **drama is creative.**

Challenging

Benjamin Bloom identified a stepped series of cognitive activity, moving from what we already know (lower) to a final evaluation phase (higher). It's known as Bloom's Taxonomy. A drama-based activity encourages students to move from lower to higher levels of cognitive activity. It challenges their brains to progress in learning.

How does that work?
Let's imagine that a class of students is asked to produce, in groups of four, a piece of drama illustrating the plight of child chimney sweeps in Victorian England. Page 13 shows how it might develop, using the structure of Bloom's Taxonomy:

Evaluation

Synthesis

Analysis

Application

Comprehension

Knowledge

Challenging

Step 1: **Knowledge**   Recall of information from history lessons/Oliver Twist/
                             TV documentaries/anecdotes

Step 2: **Comprehension**   Understanding the issues of exploitation/suitability of
                             children for the task/risks/child labour

Step 3: **Application**   Devising a series of scenes that illustrates the issues

Step 4: **Analysis**   Thinking about the available drama resources: words,
                             body language, space, characterisation, etc

Step 5: **Synthesis**   Sequencing the scenes/climax/ending

Step 6: **Evaluation**   Self- and peer-evaluation of performance

Clearly, for such challenging learning to take place, a **supportive** and **secure** learning
environment needs to be created. More of this later.

Student-centred

Drama is nothing if not student-centred.

Every student comes to the learning activity with:

- **Knowledge** – although it may be mistaken or misguided
- **Skills** – finely or barely honed
- **Attitudes** – both positive and negative

Drama techniques enable students to:

- **Choose** the direction of learning
- **Explore** the possibilities
- **Build** on what is created

Collaborative

A drama-based activity is a **TOGETHER** way of learning:

TOGETHER to engage with different personal perceptions and values
TOGETHER to listen to and challenge one another
TOGETHER to explore new horizons
TOGETHER to negotiate compromises and the best fit
TOGETHER to provide mutual support
TOGETHER to give feedback and review
TOGETHER to create synergy

Individually, students are enriched as they contend with alternatives. When a supportive group is created, conflicts of ideas can be synthesised and adapted. Students feel able to take risks in their learning, exploring new and challenging approaches. Younger children particularly enjoy the reassurance of being part of a group.

Rewarding

Participating in drama is rewarding.

1. Every group member can achieve a measure of **success** in drama. There's no one correct answer. It's more like the exploration of a desert island. Everyone can present some aspect of their discovery: their shell, flower, contorted branch, fruit, birdsong or pebble.

2. There's the personal satisfaction of **creating**. Each group unwraps an undiscovered feature, a perspective slightly different from other groups.

3. Performance evokes a natural **reward**:

 Spontaneous **applause**

 Appropriate **laughter** (or silence)

 Words of **congratulation**

To this you can add your own **public recognition** and **affirmation**.

Unleashing the caged beast

So far, so good. But maybe you're still feeling diffident about using drama-based activities. Do you feel a little like the lion-tamer as the cage door opens and the magnificent beast prowls around the ring?

Look at it this way: drama activities encourage the brain to do what it does best, ie respond to and make sense of a complicated world of emotions and ideas. So it's definitely worth entering the ring if the educational reward is sufficiently high.

Remember too, the lion-tamer has control. His top hat, red jacket and whip allow him to orchestrate the beast's behaviour. So, too, with drama activities: there are structures, techniques and tricks adaptable to most learning situations.

So why not try one for size?

A wardrobe of drama techniques

The next chapters offer seven banks of techniques for you to sample and explore:

Drama Games – starter activities to establish routines and warm up brains and bodies
Narrative – exploring the stages of a story, process or event
Character – peeling the layers of the onion
Stylisation – freeze frames, slow motion, mime and sound effects
Analogies – 'to put it another way'
Dilemmas and options – demonstrating choice and opinion
Teacher in role and using props – you assume the role of a fictional or real-life
character using real or imagined objects to re-enact events

As you navigate the book you'll find the Drama Games section organised according to
how much space you have to work in, and the other sections organised around
curriculum clusters.

Drama as Active Learning

 Drama Games ◀

 Narrative

 Character

 Stylisation

 Analogies

 Dilemmas and Options

 Teacher in Role and Using Props

Drama Games

What, why and when?

Drama games work best at the start of a lesson, as a way of preparing students for learning. They can be active and noisy but they don't need to be. They may require physical effort and/or verbal dexterity, speed and/or concentration, memory and/or good timing. The main requirement is that **they get students' attention** and are fun!

You can use games for:

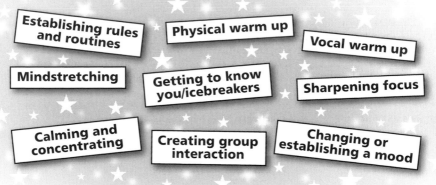

Establishing rules and routines

Physical warm up

Vocal warm up

Mindstretching

Getting to know you/icebreakers

Sharpening focus

Calming and concentrating

Creating group interaction

Changing or establishing a mood

So what's the benefit?

Since games are fun activities, they help establish a **safe**, emotionally **warm learning environment** and create a **positive relationship** with the teacher. This is no less true in secondary school environments than primary.

Games are usually **short** and **manageable** and easily incorporated into a lesson. They are high gain activities that needn't impinge on the main block of time.

All the games suggested here have potential for imaginative variations across the curriculum. They're grouped according to location, starting with simple games to play at the desk or table, progressing to games that can be played at the front of the room or in smallish spaces, then on to circle games and, finally, more energetic games that require the wide-open space of a hall or studio.

If you feel a little apprehensive, games are **an easy way for YOU to start using drama techniques**. Why not start with those that don't require you to move the furniture or to re-locate to the hall?

At the desk

High fives – (This simple routine for gaining pupils' attention can be used both at the start and at other points in the lesson.) Allow students to enter the room and unpack their bags. When you raise your open hand, students must stop what they're doing, be silent and copy the raised hand, giving you their total attention. Aim for a target response time – Years 5 and 6 respond well to this – or a simple forfeit for the last student to copy the high fives.

Ways to say hello – a game for ensuring focus. While taking a class register, students respond to their name by each choosing a different form of greeting. They can use other languages, colloquial phrases, historical forms, etc. None can be repeated. (It's helpful to read names in an *apparently* random order, ensuring that able students participate last.)

At the desk

Writing game – as an easily-managed physical warm up ask students to write their names in the air in front of them using a finger. Introduce more and more complex variations, eg they must write with their elbow/nose/backside, with their wrong hand, with both hands together, backwards, upside down, etc.

Maria, Maria, Maria – a game for sharpening focus. Say the name of a student three times (clearly and not too quickly). The student must respond by saying their name once before you complete the third time.

I went to market – a memory game. There are many variants of this game which is a good way of raising attention levels. The first student starts: *'I went to market and I bought a...'* (names item). A second student continues: *'I went to market and I bought a...'* (names item from first student) *'and a...'* (names additional item). The game continues around the group, increasing in difficulty as more items must be remembered. You need to establish a starting point and a clear route around the class.

At the desk

Countries (or names of historical characters/elements/sports stars, etc) – use this game as a mental warm-up. A first student names a country. A second student names, within a given countdown, a country beginning with the last letter of the previous country. (As with 'I went to market' you need to establish a starting point and a clear route around the class.) In this game it's impossible for students to plan ahead. The countdown adds playful pressure but can be omitted.

1, 2, 3 count – a game to encourage spontaneous teamwork. Students stand at their places. The object is for students to count to their total class number in an unplanned sequence. One student only may say each number, then sit down. If more than one student speaks at the same time, the sequence must start again. (Not as easy as it sounds!)

At the desk

Smile – a game for creating a relaxed and warm classroom atmosphere. Students stand at their places. You move amongst them, wearing a variety of unusual facial expressions. The object is for students to keep a straight face as you move around, looking at them. If they smile, they are out and must sit down until all are eliminated. Children as young as five or six really enjoy this game.

At the front of the room

Drama games need not involve all students at once. You can set up a head-to-head contest with volunteers coming to the front of the room. When one student is eliminated a replacement is chosen. The games below all encourage mental agility.

Alternate words – a pair of students creates a story, each student saying alternate words. (Instead of a word, an appropriate piece of punctuation may be offered.) Hesitation or nonsensical words result in elimination.

ABC – a pair of students holds a conversation, each successive sentence starting with the next letter of the alphabet. (eg **A**re you well?. **B**etter than I was. **C**an't complain myself. **D**aughter doing well?) Hesitation results in elimination.

At the front of the room

Questions game – two students hold a conversation using only questions. Using a statement or repeating a question means elimination. (Try a police officer and a driver, a shopkeeper and a customer, a headteacher and a student)

You can use games like this as team challenges, with points for eliminating an opponent, or try them with the whole class, pairing students at desks or tables.

In a circle

Circles are inclusive structures. Everyone has eye contact with each other and the space is shared equally without barriers between members. Students can remain in their places for word games or they can be encouraged to move.

Talking stick – to help establish the discipline of listening to one speaker at a time, students sit in a discussion circle and are allowed to speak only when they hold the talking stick (provide a suitable prop) which is given by you. Those who speak out of turn pay a simple forfeit. This works very well in primary classrooms where children are attentive self-policers.

All change if... – students sit in a circle on chairs. One student stands at the centre. The centre student says, *'All change if...'* and gives a category (eg ...you have a pet/support Spurs/hate peas, etc). Students fitting the category swap places while the centre student tries to steal a place. The last student standing goes into the centre.

In a circle

Put a name on it – there are two intentions with this game: to practise names and to create a smooth passing of the ball around the group. Make catching easy, not difficult! Students stand in a circle, with you at the centre holding a tennis ball. You say a student's name (eg Lisa) and throw the ball to Lisa who catches it. Lisa says the name of another student (eg Tom) and throws the ball, which is caught by Tom. The game continues until all students have been involved at least once.

The magic object – a good way to stimulate the visual imagination. Place a simple prop (stick, bucket, hoop, ball, rope) in the centre of the circle. Students enter the circle one at a time, pick up the object and say *'This is not a stick (bucket, hoop, etc), it's a...'* then name a creative option, eg, a javelin, helmet, halo, etc and mime the object in use. Encourage students to take leaps of imagination.

In a circle

The games on this page are fast-moving and provide a controlled physical warm up.

Reactor – half the class sit in a circle on chairs. The remainder stand, hands behind backs, behind the seated students,. You stand at the centre of the circle and say a seated student's name. That student has to get out of their chair and tick your back before their partner can do the same to them. If ticked they take your place in the centre. (Emphasise the difference between a tick and a slap!)

Fruit salad (or a variation, eg chemical elements, football clubs, currencies) – students sit in a circle on chairs, one student standing in the middle. Give everyone a name (pear, apple, cherry, melon, peach), repeating the sequence around the circle. Next, say the name of a fruit from the sequence. Students with that name must swap places across the circle while the one in the middle tries to take one of their places. If successful, they take over that name and the beaten student goes to the centre.

Circles are easily created with a small amount of classroom reorganisation. Once formed, they can provide a variation on group dynamics for discussion tasks.

In a wide open space

You may occasionally have access to a studio or hall for a workshop session. The following games make use of space. These three are all good physical warm ups:

Human Lego – in groups, using only their bodies, students create models (static or moving) of objects you suggest, eg elephant, cuckoo clock, firework display. This game works well across the age range from Year 4 onwards.

Sequences – the class must form, as quickly as possible, the sequence you name, eg height order/age order/alphabetical order by first or second name, etc.

Machines – groups create a machine for a purpose, eg a nappy-changing machine, an elephant-washing machine, a bridge-building machine. Encourage sound effects.

In a wide open space

The two games below help create a concentrated yet relaxed movement out of which other games can proceed

Neutral walk – students walk at a medium pace in random directions. They look ahead, using peripheral vision to avoid colliding. No communication with eyes or voice is allowed. (This stimulates creativity.)

Enemies and friends – students begin the neutral walk. In their minds only, they must each choose a member of the class as their enemy. They stay as far away from this person as possible without the person knowing. Students then choose a second class member as their friend. They continue walking, keeping their friend between them and their enemy, without either knowing.

In a wide open space

Amoeba race – this physical warm-up game takes the form of a relay race so needs a very large space. Students form two equal teams, which divide into threes. Trios hold hands to form a small circle. Each trio completes their leg of the relay then hands over to the next trio in their team.

Instant improvisations – as a way of stimulating the imaginative use of voice and gesture divide the class into two groups A and B. Start the neutral walk and tell students that when you stop them you will announce two characters, one for A, the other for B. Students must find a partner from the opposite group and immediately begin to improvise a piece of drama. Allow the drama to develop for 20 – 30 seconds then resume the neutral walk. Stop the students again and announce a different pair of characters. Repeat the sequence four or five times. (Suitable pairs might be: millionaire/shoplifter, lost child/police officer, tourist/tramp, cowboy/punk rocker, etc).

Classroom management

Before
- Launch a game quickly. It's the hook to engage students' attention
- Have resources in place, space organised and a simple explanation of the rules
- Ensure there is a large enough area available for safe game play

During
- Have a clear mechanism for gaining students' attention without needing to shout, eg a countdown from five to zero, a raised hand, or finger on lips that students must copy in silence. They must respond immediately, quietly passing the word
- Ensure there are no long-term losers in the game. Bend the rules a little

After
- Keep the momentum. Allow a moment of transition for students to regain their breath then give a clear, defined introduction for the next activity. Students should be in an alert frame of mind, ready to respond
- Keep a bank of popular games to use as a reward in the last few minutes of a successful lesson

Drama as Active Learning

 Drama Games

 Narrative ◄

 Character

 Stylisation

 Analogies

 Dilemmas and Options

 Teacher in Role and Using Props

Narrative

Navigating the ideas

In this section and most of the following sections, you'll find that once the **techniques** have been explained and illustrated, **ideas** to spark the imagination are arranged in **curriculum clusters**:

 Literature

 Music, Art and Design

 Science
(with Maths ideas
where appropriate)

 Modern Foreign Languages

 PE and Sport

 Social Sciences
(Geography, Sociology
and Psychology)

 Humanities (History and RE)

Glance through the ideas in all clusters. Many can easily be adapted for other subjects. Occasionally, if the drama technique in question doesn't lend itself naturally to the subjects, a cluster will not appear. Though if you're very imaginative…!

What is narrative?

Essentially, a narrative is an account of a series of events. It occurs in many forms within the curriculum. For instance:

Story – eg literary fiction and non-fiction
Sequence – eg the phases of a triple jump in athletics or the 2x table
Process – eg a chemical experiment containing a reaction
Procedure – eg the passage of a Bill through the Commons and Lords
Flow chart – eg how to use an internet search engine
Instructions – eg a cookery recipe

With drama techniques it's possible to enact these series of events in a multi-sensory, active way. Restating the narrative both reinforces the sequence of events and gives the brain another way to assimilate it.

Try using narrative techniques at the start of a lesson to **review** previously learned processes, sequences or story lines. Alternatively, at the end of a lesson they can help to **reinforce** what has been learned.

Technique 1: Storyboard

For many students, producing a simple storyboard (a series of cartoon images) of a narrative sequence is a helpful way of pinning down a narrative. This can be drawn but is just as easily reproduced physically by a group of students as a series of still images or tableaux (pages 71-72), providing a visual point of reference.

Like this: The Boscastle flood

A series of 6 images is needed for a front page newspaper article about the destruction of Boscastle in Cornwall by a flash flood. Students, in groups of four or five, produce six physical still images, eg:

- In the pub before the flood
- Hearing a warning
- Sandbagging the door
- A person swept away
- Rescuing an elderly person
- Reactions the next day

A physical storyboard can be a strong way to start a lesson, a useful jumping off point for a range of written, drawn and improvised drama tasks.

Technique 2: Mime

While some students find it easy to memorise a word-based list or sequence, others benefit from a kinaesthetic approach.

Like this: 👉 Mountain erosion

Students in groups of four or five devise a simple mimed sequence to illustrate the five main factors causing erosion in upland areas:

- Wind – flap arms
- Rain – ripple fingers
- Ice and frost – hug self
- Sheep farming – down on all fours
- Tourism – tramp vigorously

The mime can be realistic or metaphorical. What matters is that the students 'anchor' the sequence to the actions they choose.

Technique 3: Commentary

Describing a sequence of events helps to imprint it on the mind. To encourage creativity, instead of a straight description, ask students to use a style of commentary, (eg sports match, game show, home improvements, etc).

Like this: John Donne's poem, *The Flea* (style: boxing match)
Year 11 students prepare scripts along the following lines:

> *'Welcome to this important fixture. At stake is the virtue of the young lady in the pink corner. She's a newcomer with a reputation for a firm mind. In the blue corner, however, the defending champion, Donne, is confident of a swift victory.*
>
> *Round 1. An assertive start by Donne. That word 'mark' is powerful and aggressive. He has the upper hand already. How will his opponent respond?'* etc

A development of this technique would be a relay of commentators. You stop the commentary and nominate a student to continue from their script. Very able students may be able to create a commentary spontaneously.

Technique 4: Perspectives

A narrative can be seen from many different points of view, both in terms of proximity and of personal involvement. Try cutting from one descriptive viewpoint to another in a kind of counterpoint.

Like this: The Battle of the Somme

Three students describe the first day of the battle:

- From British high command 10 miles behind the lines
- As a German soldier looking over the top
- As a rat in a British bunker

Primary age children particularly respond to using similes in their description: *'I can see a tree with no leaves, like a skeleton'*.

To involve more students, try the relay technique suggested on the previous page.

Technique 5: Cause and effect

Each part of a sequence is both caused by and is the cause of other parts of the chain. To help establish the relationship of events in a sequence, begin at the conclusion and work backwards, identifying every possible cause.

Like this: Analysis of 100 metres performance

'I came 3rd in my race with a very slow time...

...because I couldn't sustain my speed

...because my shoulder muscles were not relaxed

...because my energy was concentrated in swinging my arms...' etc

Students love to apply their ingenuity in this technique, identifying small but significant causal factors. They may wish to work in pairs when engaged in personal analysis, whereas a more objective analysis, eg a chemical reaction, can be a whole class activity.

So what's the benefit?

Narrative techniques allow you to focus on significant **events, encounters or phases** within a sequence. By breaking something down into its composite elements and dramatising it, you can:

- **Examine** each narrative element separately
- **Consider** the effect of intervention at key points
- **Hypothesise** alternative outcomes

Storytelling is also a valuable **memory aid**. Inanimate or mechanical processes from maths, science and technology are sometimes more easily remembered if restated in the form of a story.

Literature – ideas

These techniques help students identify and familiarise themselves with the structure of events in fiction and non-fiction texts:

1 Three students give versions of a key scene in a novel, one as a participant in the scene, one as an observer close to the action, one as a distant observer.

2 Students repeat a plot line backwards as cause and effect. The logic of the narrative is clarified.

3 A TV journalist gives an on-the-spot commentary on the deaths of Tybalt and Mercutio in Act 3, Scene 1 of *Romeo and Juliet*.

4 Students in small groups prepare a high-speed mimed summary of a plot line.

5 Using five still images, students illustrate key scenes from a biography.

Music, art and design – ideas

❶ After listening to sections of a piece of music, to identify tone students provide a storyline that links them. They then create a series of tableaux (see pages 71-72) that tell the story.

❷ Students view a painting created in a narrative style (Pre-Raphaelite paintings are a good source). To provide a sense of context, in groups they produce scenes that took place before and after the moment portrayed. Students are encouraged to examine visual clues.

❸ Students as DJs create a radio programme that illustrates the development of a style of music (eg blues, reggae, dance music). The show consists of four music tracks and a carefully scripted commentary. A useful summative activity.

❹ To memorise the code of practice for using a piece of technology equipment students create a mime sequence (eg tie back long hair/tuck in tie/wear apron and goggles/ensure work is securely clamped, etc). This could be a mime adaptation of the game 'I went to market' (page 23).

Science – ideas

Stories as memory aids are particularly helpful when dealing with scientific processes. Use circles of students to develop the following:

1 Use a version of 'I went to market' (page 23) to review an experiment, eg: *'I took a test tube and in it placed 10 grammes of…./I took a test tube, in it placed 10 grammes of… and clamped it over the burner/I took a test tube, in it placed 10 grammes of…, clamped it over the burner and heated it to X ° centigrade…'* etc.

2 A creative way to remember chemical symbols is to invent stories and characters: Mr. and Mrs. Hydrogen and their daughter Oxygen (H_2O) dropped in to meet Mr. Copper, his partner Sulphur and their four children, each also surprisingly called Oxygen ($CuSO_4$). When they met…

3 The class produces a mime in which a student representing the raw material bauxite is passed through an industrial process that eventually turns him/her into an aluminium pan. Groups represent different stages in the process and 'mould' the student appropriately.

Modern foreign languages – ideas

Storytelling is a useful activity for using new vocabulary and language features. It also gives students the opportunity to use a variety of tenses.

1 In groups of three, students examine a magazine picture and prepare short descriptions as if one is very close, one near to and one far away from the action.

2 As a TV journalist, prepare the script of a commentary on a famous national event – the liberation of Paris, the destruction of the Berlin Wall, etc.

3 Students each provide an amusing family photo. A partner invents a short explanation of what caused the amusement. This can be a prepared written piece or a spontaneous response depending on student ability.

PE and sport – ideas

❶ Technical events, particularly in athletics, can be broken down into component still images. Ask students in groups of four to isolate body positions:

- To produce a competent shot putt, discus or javelin throw
- For a high jump run up
- For the phases of the triple jump

Similar breakdowns can be produced of a tennis serve, a forehand or backhand shot; a rugby pass, a series of dance steps. By creating a narrative sequence, students concentrate on body position stage by stage, helping balance and focusing the direction of power.

❷ A match debrief in any sport can contain short narrative accounts from different perspectives (eg keeper, midfield, attack). By assessing in terms of the whole game rather than individual moments, students become aware of the overall rhythm.

❸ Use the 'cause and effect' technique on page 42.

Social sciences – ideas

These are all summative activities and good examples of how drama techniques can reinforce learning:

1 Students create four action scenes (20 seconds each) to illustrate what happens in an Asian village before, during, one week after, and one year after a tsunami.

2 Students give a guided tour commentary of a thought process to illustrate how the brain works. Data visits the Reptilian Brain, Limbic System and Neo-cortex as if on a holiday tour.

3 A living cartoon strip – students tell the story of the fight for women's emancipation in six still pictures.

4 Students as TV chefs produce multi-decker sandwiches.
Each layer (give ingredients) represents a geological era.
Different students can add each new layer.

Humanities – ideas

1 You interview students as characters present at the birth of Jesus (Mary/wise man/shepherd/sheep or ox, etc) viewing the narrative from different perspectives.

2 As a memory aid, tell Buddhism's Eightfold Path as a story involving Homer Simpson: *'Homer had trouble understanding rightly because he…. He sometimes didn't take the right action towards his children because he…'* etc. Different students must recount different steps from the path.

3 Students tell the story of Henry VIII's wives in the style of different TV shows (try Eastenders/You've Been Framed/Men Behaving Badly/Blind Date).

4 Following detailed preparation, the battle of Agincourt is re-enacted in the style of a war game. Two able students, with appropriate maps and notes to hand, are the opposing leaders. The rest of the class are the different types of soldiers and must move as their leaders direct.

Character

Exploring character

Many students enjoy narrative because it moves quickly. They race along with the story but can sometimes be left with a superficial understanding, particularly in perception of character.

Children are also influenced by the stereotypical style of much TV drama characterisation, where the 'goodies' and 'baddies' are easily distinguished, and undeveloped stock characters prevail.

The techniques in this section encourage students to explore the complexities of individual character by considering for example:

- **Frame of mind** – conflict is more common than certainty and motivation is usually mixed
- **Dialogue** – what someone says may not be what they are thinking, what they intended to say, what they actually communicate
- **Morality** – the goodies and the baddies are sometimes indistinguishable

Uses and benefits

There are numerous applications for the ideas in this section. Try using them:

- To gain insight into the motivation and personality of historical characters
- To illustrate the moral uncertainty that lies behind many political, business and scientific decisions (eg animal experimentation)
- To explore the rounded personality of a fictional character (though beware of going beyond the author's intention)

You can also apply these ideas metaphorically to inanimate objects. A mountain, a tennis racquet or a type of timber has characteristics that distinguish it from other mountains, racquets and timber (just think of the mystique attached to wines). The 'character' techniques in this section can be used to illustrate what makes the inanimate world tick.

Technique 1: Role on the wall

On a large sheet of paper draw a life-size outline of a body, representing the character. Students stand inside the body and voice or write information about internal influences on that character, eg personality, motives and beliefs. Around the body outline they should voice or write a contrasting set of information, eg the character's external influences such as relationships, social and religious circumstances and expectations. The visual record can be kept as a useful display.

Like this: Willy Loman in Arthur Miller's *Death of a Salesman*
- Internal influences to write inside the body shape could include: guilt, age, jealousy, personal dream, etc
- External influences to write around the body shape could be: market forces, change, Biff, Linda, etc

Ask students to make the outline – one lies down while another draws around them. Primary children in particular love to create things BIG.

Technique 2: Gossip circle

Gossip circle is a quick way to summarise what a group knows or has learnt about a character. Able students can expand on the more basic responses of weaker members of the group.

Choose four students who sit in a circle. In turn, students give information about a character, using evidence from previous learning or from the given text. They do not repeat the previous student's ideas but may choose to expand on them. Continue the process around the circle until ideas run out.

Like this: Siddharta Gautama (The Buddha)

1. Siddharta Gautama grew up in a palace.
2. He saw four sights.
3. One of these was an old man.
4. The other three were sickness, death and a holy man.
5. His father prevented him from seeing these things in the palace ...etc.

Technique 3: Alter ego

Students work in pairs with each pair representing a single character. Student 1 speaks and acts as the public face of a character. This may be an extract from the script of a play, an interview, part of an improvised dialogue, etc. Student 2 presents the thoughts of that same character, ironically commenting or even contradicting.

| Like this: | Father of the bride's wedding speech:

Student 1: *'I'd like to welcome you here on this happy occasion.'*
Student 2: *'I wouldn't have invited half of you. Certainly not Robert and Jane. They never invited us to their son's wedding.'*

Student 1: *'I'm sure you'll agree with me that the bride looks radiant today.'*
Student 2: *'She's concealed the pregnancy very well.'*

Student 1: *'And she's found herself a fine husband.'*
Student 2: *'I'll have to make sure I rewrite the will, without his name on it…'* etc.

This is a rewarding technique, often revealing a significant sub-text to the public voice.

Technique 4: Status levels

Students take the role of characters in a narrative or dialogue and assume positions that indicate the level of status or power of their character in relation to others. A selection of positions might be: lying on the floor, sitting on the floor, sitting on a chair, standing on the floor, standing on a chair etc. Students change position as character interaction develops.

Like this: The life story of Martin Luther King
One student represents Martin Luther King. Others are groups or individuals with whom he interacted (Ku Klux Klan, the President, Black Power movement, Coretta King, white liberals, the church, etc).

In groups students choose four moments in Martin Luther King's life. For each they create a still image assuming positions that illustrate levels of status or power between people. The rest of the class can analyse and challenge the group's choice of status levels using previous learning to justify their comments.

Technique 5: Hot-seating

Place a chair at the front of the class. This is the hot seat. A student sits in the hot seat, and responds in role to prepared or spontaneous questions posed by the class. These may be factual questions to test accuracy of recall or expansive questions to develop character analysis.

Like this: Student in role of French vineyard owner (factual)
- Name two types of grape you grow.
- Name the disease that nearly destroyed the wine industry.
- Name a famous wine-growing area in France.

Or: Student in role of Artful Dodger in *Oliver Twist* (expansive)
- Why do you fear an old man like Fagin?
- Have you ever been caught? How did you feel?
- Who's the more skilful criminal, Fagin or Bill Sykes?

Given that students love to put one another on the spot, this familiar technique is still one of the best for encouraging class involvement.

Technique 6: Thought-tracking

Freeze the action during a narrative (this could be an improvised drama, a DVD of a typical day in the life of an Amazonian Indian, the reading of a novel, etc) and single out a character. You then nominate students to voice the thoughts of characters within the narrative.

Since you are nominating students you can ensure that everyone participates. Begin with those students who can make a simple response, encouraging contrasting sets of thoughts from later contributors.

Like this: While watching a DVD on the history of nuclear energy
Students voice the thoughts of characters, eg:
- A scientist involved in splitting the atom
- The pilot of the Enola Gay at the moment of dropping the bomb on Hiroshima
- The present French president

Technique 7: SWOT

Divide the class into four groups representing **S**trengths, **W**eaknesses, **O**pportunities and **T**hreats. Name a controversial issue (eg wind farms, the penalty shoot-out, lowering the age of sexual consent to 14). Each group discusses the issue from their SWOT perspective and produces a 60 second statement summarising their views. A student in role as an expert presents the statement to the class.

Like this: The penalty shoot-out
S – gives a clear result, exciting
W – not a team activity, artificial, destroys reputations
O – suggest alternative ways to decide a result
T – influence of advertisers, marketing

A SWOT exercise is useful for clarifying issues to ensure a balanced discussion. By concentrating on one element students are encouraged to create detailed arguments.

Technique 8: Entrances and exits

Whenever a real or fictional character enters or exits a narrative, ask students in role as the character to answer the following questions:

When a character enters:
- Where have I come from?
- How do I feel?
- What do I want?

As a character exits:
- Where am I going?
- How do I feel?
- What have I achieved

The answers highlight how every character has both a past and a future and, because of their simplicity, the questions can easily be answered by young children.

Like this: 👉

Winston Churchill at the start and finish of WW2; Billy Caspar at the close of *Kestrel for a Knave*; Alfred Nobel (the inventor of high explosive) on his death bed; characters entering the factory in *Charlie and the Chocolate Factory*.

Literature – ideas

❶ Role on the wall – for a character study. Inside the body write (or collage) internal influences (personality, motives). Outside write external influences (relationships, social and religious expectations, etc). The drawing can be displayed in the room as an aide memoir.

❷ Gossip circle – to review what has been discovered about a fictional character.

❸ Alter ego – in play-reading each character has a partner that voices the character's thoughts throughout the dialogue. Thought-tracking would be a variation on this that involves the whole class.

❹ Status levels – in play-reading the 'characters' must also use levels. Encourage students to change levels frequently to illustrate subtle relationship shifts.

❺ Hot-seat an author about the way they see a character.

❻ Use the SWOT technique to produce a 4-part character study.

Music, art and design – ideas

1 Hot-seating – after listening to a music extract, students are interviewed in the hot seat as instruments that were used. Class ask questions about contribution of instrument. Nominate instruments before listening to focus students' attention.

2 Role on the wall – the key character is an artist, musician or designer. Detail their internal influences and that of the society in which they lived.

3 Students represent instruments in a band or orchestra. As music is played they must assume status levels according to their prominence in the musical mix.

4 Thought-tracking – students focus on figures in a painting or sculpture and voice what they imagine the character might be thinking.

5 Use a variation on the SWOT technique to comment on a piece of visual art (strengths/weaknesses/additions I would make/elements I would remove).

Science – ideas

1 Hot-seating – to revise factual information (eg properties of chemical elements/planets/organs of the body, etc). Student in the hot seat represents an element/planet/organ and is quizzed by the class on a true/false basis.

2 Role on the wall – the body is that of a famous scientist. Students in turn stand inside the body shape to state the positive contribution made by the scientist, outside the body shape to state problems and dilemmas that have been caused.

3 SWOT exercise – name a controversial scientific issue (eg stem cell research) and ask students in groups to prepare a statement.

Modern foreign languages – ideas

1 Use hot-seating to encourage conversational language and the construction of questions. Less able students will be able to compose one question each without threat. More able students will respond to the challenge of unexpected questions as they talk about themselves.

2 Alter ego – pair two more able with two less able students. Less able students conduct a conversation while more able students voice their thoughts.

3 Gossip circle – a (willing) student sits in the centre of a circle. Class members in turn create a fictional gossip portrait of the student. Emphasise that gossip must not be malicious or hurtful!

PE and sport – ideas

1 Hot-seating – as a combination of self- and peer-assessment, students are hot-seated regarding their performance in the class activity.

2 Thought-tracking – occasionally in a game freeze the play and ask students to think about the options available to the player with the ball. Encourage evaluation of all options and project the consequences. This will encourage strategic thinking.

3 Role on the wall – a student lies on the floor within the body shape. The class gives peer assessment of performance, standing over or next to the body as appropriate. Aim to balance negative comments with positive comments.

4 SWOT – divide a team into four groups for a quick debrief after a match.

Social sciences – ideas

1 To revise learning on indigenous peoples, hot-seat representatives of different age groups and genders from that people. Concentrate on revealing feelings.

2 Thought-tracking – students watch video footage of a catastrophic event (tsunami/earthquake/hurricane) observing the effect on people. Re-run the video, freezing at key points. Students take on roles of people they see and voice what they feel physically and what they are thinking.

3 Role on the wall – choose a controversial psychologist (eg Freud) and examine their positive and negative influence on society.

4 Thought-tracking – take a picture image that illustrates a sociological issue and project this onto a whiteboard. Students in turn stand alongside the image and voice what they think the people in the image are feeling/wanting to do/hoping, etc.

Humanities – ideas

1 A student sits in the hot seat as a character from history and responds to questions from the class.

2 Role on the wall – the body represents Jesus. Divide students into groups representing different types of people he met (Romans/Jewish scholars/ women/children, etc.). Each student walks to the body and expresses how they feel about Jesus.

3 Thought-tracking – students recreate an illustration of a historical or religious event. Individuals choose a character and voice what the character is thinking at that moment.

4 Gossip circle – revise a key person's biography by students in turn each contributing a piece of information.

Drama as Active Learning

 Drama Games

 Narrative

 Character

 Stylisation

 Analogies

 Dilemmas and Options

 Teacher in Role and Using Props

Stylisation

What is it?

Stylisation is drama stripped down to its basic components.

Each is used by itself:

(from stillness to exaggerated in pace or style)   as an inanimate building block

Technique 1: Still image/tableau

A frozen moment in time is reproduced by an individual or group and held for up to a count of 10. The technique is more easily illustrated than explained. Think of a photograph, a sculpture, a painting or a cartoon frame.

| Like this: | a painting entitled *The execution of Charles I*

Student 1 is Charles kneeling at the block
Student 2 is the executioner, axe raised
Student 3 is Oliver Cromwell, suitably grim but pleased
Student 4 is another Parliamentarian, uncertain about the execution

The class can analyse the visual signals given in the still image. Are they 'correct'?

Still images can also be sequenced to produce a simple narrative. One group can produce the whole sequence or groups can take one frame each. (Remind students to choose positions they can hold in balance for the required time.)

Technique 1: Still image/tableau (cont'd)

Still images are useful ways of exploring emotions or concepts. Being asked to produce tableaux that depict, say, jealousy, rage, anxiety, power, citizenship is challenging and thought provoking for pupils of both primary and secondary age.

There are numerous developments from still image that can provide variety:

Human sculpture

A pair of student volunteers comes to the front of the class. One is the sculptor, the other the clay. You give a title for a sculpture (eg 'Macbeth gone mad'). The sculptor moves the student clay into an appropriate stance. Other students may assume the role of sculptor and improve the image in the light of previous learning.

Sociogram

You give the class a title (eg 'Reborn') and invite students one by one to become part of the image. The first may be a girl cradling her newborn child. A boy may lie as a dead body behind her. A third is a priest making the sign of the cross over the body. Allow the image to build until natural completion is reached.

Technique 2: Mime

It's useful to work in silence at points in a lesson. Voices tend to compete for attention and volume levels rise. Mime encourages students to communicate solely through gesture, facial expression and body language and can often encourage involvement by those whose language skills are more limited.

Like this: under-age drinking

In small groups students produce short mime sketches to illustrate the pressure for teenagers to drink alcohol under-age. Examples might be: advertising, older friends, unsupervised parties, need for a boy/girl friend.

Encourage students who have some facility with visual communication techniques such as Makaton® or British Sign Language to incorporate these into their drama.

Technique 3: Soundtrack

This is the converse of mime: no movement, only sound. This can be words and/or noises. It's particularly suited to those students who have a musical gift.

Like this: 👉 a city backstreet on a foggy winter's night
Before producing a visual piece, an art class recreates the city environment. Students sit in a circle and each chooses a sound effect from the city at night. Go round the circle with students reproducing their sounds using their voices and other bodily resources (eg fingers, hands, feet). When confident with the technique, you can put the sounds together, inviting students to participate spontaneously or orchestrating the soundtrack yourself.

During presentation observers must be totally silent to avoid distracting the performers. It's best used with students sitting in a circle as movement is minimised and sound is directed into the group.

Technique 4: Slow motion

'Slo-mo' is a useful technique for those moments, usually moments of conflict, when you sense the potential for the drama to descend into chaos. It may be a necessary fight scene such as Bill Sykes' murder of Nancy, or David slaying Goliath. It may be a point of tense conflict between rivals, or the reproduction of a complex chemical reaction. Slo-mo requires students to be controlled and precise in their actions and emphasises the heightened tension produced by a pause. Very useful with active pupils across the key stages.

Like this: Romeo's intervention and the death of Mercutio
Students in groups of three produce slo-mo mime interpretations of the fight, concentrating on how Mercutio is stabbed by Tybalt under Romeo's arm as he tries to stop the fight. There is a balletic control and precision required, which encourages boys especially to focus on subtle character portrayal rather than the more usual brute force. If you're confident, you may choose to add a soundtrack and real-life pace.

Technique 5: Physicalisation

Students use their bodies to physically portray inanimate objects, with the option of giving the objects human attributes. They can also act as pieces of human Lego, interlocking with one another to create something more complex which may be still or move like a machine.

Like this: Granny flat

Students create the environment in which an older person might live by physically portraying objects in the room. They may choose to be beneficial (a cosy armchair, a stair lift) or unhelpful (a jar with a stiff lid, a high cupboard). Each student must explain what they are and their effect on you (the very elderly teacher) who walks round the flat.

So what's the benefit?

The minimalist approach helps students pare down material to its essential elements. This can provide clarity within complexity. Also, these techniques require high levels of concentration from participants in their preparation and from the audience during presentation. Both parties need to focus on:

The Visual	**Sound**	**Movement**
Body language	Pitch	Gesture
Use of space (proxemics)	Rhythm	Expression
Expression	Volume	Direction
Relationship of bodies	Pace	Pace
		Force

Through this, students can develop a precise and clearly defined technical vocabulary that can be transferred across the curriculum into music, PE, MFL, etc.

Literature – ideas

1 Slo-mo – to help visualise a complex moment of conflict in a text (eg the death of Piggy in *Lord of the Flies*) the scene is mimed in slow motion, repeating until the class agrees on the accuracy.

2 Still images time line – summarise a character's life in six still images, each representing a key moment. Alternatively, groups produce a series of 'photographs' representing scenes from a text. Class members are challenged to recognise them.

3 Soundtrack – students summarise a scene from a play or novel in 10 lines of (not necessarily consecutive) dialogue quoted from the text.

4 Human sculpture – isolate a character at a key moment in a novel or play. Two students produce a human sculpture of the character at that moment. A development would be for pairs of students to introduce other characters, creating a group tableau.

Music, art and design – ideas

1 Still images – students in pairs or small groups create a still image reproduction of a painting. Class comments not only on accuracy but also on the effect of slight differences of interpretation.

2 Mime – in pairs or fours students create a movement or narrative sequence to illustrate the mood of an extract of music.

3 Still images – students enact a six frame tableau sequence to illustrate the production of a specific type of natural fibre. Different groups can illustrate cotton, linen, wool and silk.

4 Physicalisation – using only their bodies, students create a moving model of a loom. Encourage accuracy of direction and power of essential movements.

5 Soundtrack – in groups of four students create the conversations and sounds that are evoked by a painting or photograph.

Science – ideas

1 Mime – groups of students mime a scientific process run in reverse. A good revision activity.

2 Physicalisation – students are given roles as individual chemical molecules. They must form compounds with the correct combinations.

3 Still images SWOT gallery – in four groups students create still images that illustrate the strengths, weaknesses, opportunities and threats posed by animal experimentation (or any other controversial scientific issue).

Social sciences – ideas

1 Soundtrack – students create a soundtrack collage of the Amazon rainforest. By focusing on sound they are encouraged to consider precise details of flora, fauna and human presence from previous learning.

2 Still image – individually or in groups, students create a human sculpture to express what key words (eg family, institution, morality, childhood, etc) mean to them. Class comments on the variety of interpretation. Works just as well with A level students as with primary pupils.

3 Slo-mo dreams of urban drift – in groups, students create slow motion dream sequences representing rural people's expectations of a move to the city.

4 Sociogram – give students a theme (eg racism). One student stands or sits in space. A second student places himself or herself in relation to the first (higher/lower/back towards/near/far, etc) and explains what they signify. Third, fourth, fifth, etc students join, each giving an explanation of their relationship. End in a still image.

Humanities – ideas

1 Physicalisation – students create a model of a motte and bailey castle using only their bodies. Setting this as a whole class task lets you monitor leadership and communication skills.

2 Still image – in small groups students create a memorial to commemorate the end of a specific war. It must highlight key features of the war. An extension would be to create a memorial for the losing side or to write a speech for the unveiling.

3 Soundtrack – recreate the sounds of a Victorian street or a visit to the worship centre of a major religion.

4 Mime – as a memory aid create a series of hand gestures to recreate the sequence of actions at the Christian communion service.

Analogies

What is it?

To put it another way.....
For that's exactly what an analogy is. As far as drama techniques go, analogies ask students to transfer previous learning into another form or context. Usually the new context involves some form of presentation, such as:

- To a different audience
- Using entertainment media conventions
- Using an extended metaphor
- Creating a ritual

The learning content remains the same but, like a piece of putty, it is reshaped. This requires engagement with the content and clear understanding of its substance and form. Pages 85-93 contain a range of possible analogies, easily adapted for most subject areas.

Analogy 1: New audience

Students present what they have learned as if to a different age group (eg a younger year group or senior citizens) or to a different geographical or historical group (eg Martians or King Henry VIII and his court). They must take account of the audience's knowledge, expectations and ability.

Like this: The effects of smoking (Yr 10 students present as if to a Yr 5 audience.) Students create a presentation that uses simple language, visual humour, CBBC and Disney Channel styles and role models, yet accurately communicates the factual information. (Even better if you can invite a real Yr 5 audience to watch the presentation.)

Analogy 2: TV documentary programme

The brief is for students in groups of five or six to create a 10 minute presentation of a topic for the class in the style of a particular TV channel.

Like this: Give them a basic set of ingredients, for instance:

- Two interviews giving opposing points of view
- An expert opinion (in role)
- Re-enactment of events (mime or slo-mo)
- Photographic evidence (still images)

Make available resources such as a flip chart, OHP or PowerPoint to encourage visuals.

In my experience students respond superbly to this technique, the more creative building on the knowledge of the more academic, while less extrovert students are usually happy to read from a prepared script. But beware – someone always wants to be the camera operator!

Analogy 3: Metaphor

Find ways to re-present learning in extended metaphors that emphasise certain features:

Like this: A narrative, such as the passage of a Bill through Parliament, could become a competitive multi-sports event for which students provide a commentary.

- Problems and tensions are shown as barriers or puzzles: *'The Tories raise the bar by asking a question. How will Labour respond? The Minister runs in, he's up and he's cleared it. Can Labour find the elusive five votes they need for victory? Their supporters are well hidden but the Whips seek them out from corners and alcoves.'*
- Other characters become opponents: *'The Lib Dems are bringing on their star striker. She takes a run and hurls a question.'*
- The finishing tape is the final vote: *'We await the judges' decision: yes it's 9.9, 9.8, 9.7, 9.9 – a resounding victory.'*

Analogy 3: Metaphor (cont'd)

Be imaginative in creating metaphors. There's no end to the possibilities:

Make the inanimate human (a love story between weather systems)
Make morality into a machine (how would a greed machine behave?)
Make humans into animals (think of *Animal Farm*)
Any war can become a game (same drink, different bottle)
Any slight disagreement can become a war (each riposte is an artillery salvo)

The commentary or script shouldn't be too elaborate and does not need to be well written. Allow students about 10 minutes to prepare before selecting a few to share with the class. The learning intention is simply to give a different perspective in order to emphasise certain features and to reinforce the learning.

Analogy 4: Ceremony

Students prepare a sequence of symbolic actions and explanatory speeches that propose intentions or summarise achievements, eg:

- To mark the opening of a significant building, eg Caernarfon Castle
- To mark the end of an era, eg the death of Queen Victoria
- To inaugurate a venture, eg Sir John Hunt's Everest expedition in 1953

Like this: The opening of Europe's largest wind farm
- Some students prepare speeches for participants such as the Prime Minister, the head of Greenpeace and the local Mayor
- Others write poems on behalf of the Poet Laureate
- A dance group prepares a piece of symbolic dance 'The Spirit of the Wind'
- These are put in sequence, culminating in the cutting of the ribbon

This is an excellent way to wrap up a topic.

Analogy 5: Ritual

To revise work on a specific cultural or geographical group, students prepare a sequence of actions and words that typifies the group and illustrates their values. This might be a ritual for dawn or sunset, to invoke a blessing, or to ward off evil. Ingredients of the ritual could include:

- Repeated actions
- Chants
- Prayers
- Bathing

- Circles
- Dance
- Sacrifice

Like this: Morning ritual for 1960s hippies (gender: male)
The following are organised into a repeated sequence:
- Actions: give a peace sign, sit cross-legged on the floor, smoke a joint, dance in a circle
- Chanted words: *'yeah man'*, *'groovy'*, *'let it all hang out'*, *'make love not war'*

Ask students about the leader of the ritual. How is he/she chosen? Encourage them to think of gender and status issues.

Analogy 6: Advert

A succinct presentation encourages students to remember the key features of the learning. Ask students to devise a 60 second advert to promote a product, a lifestyle, a political party or an opinion they have learned about. Give the main ingredients:

- A single idea to communicate
- Catchy slogan (use rhyme, alliteration)
- Voxpop (one sentence interviews on the street)
- Visual engagement
- Humour

Like this: The Fosbury Flop

- Promoting the Fosbury Flop as a style of high jumping
- Slogan – 'Fly high with the Flop' (repeated in the background)
- Vox pop – brief interviews with three athletes about the advantages of the technique
- 4-phase still image sequence of the technique
- Exaggerated mime of athlete receiving gold medal

Analogy 7: Quiz show

As a summative task, try using a quiz show for a framework. Many formats are possible. Ask your students for the latest suggestions. Educational websites (see below) also have sets of questions and interactive models that can be shown on an interactive whiteboard.

Students should write their own sets of questions from their learning. Make sure they spend as much time on the learning-related questions as they do on building the quiz show context. It's easy to focus on the wrapping rather than the content.

Be aware of the competitive element. Sometimes use teams so everyone has a chance to be a winner, but also allow for individual excellence to be demonstrated on other occasions.

Like this:

www.teachingandlearningresources.co.uk (*Who wants to be a Millionaire*)
www.schoolhistory.co.uk (Create your own quiz)
Or type *'make your own quiz game'* into www.google.co.uk for many up-to-date resources.

Analogy 8: Human gallery

Using techniques from the Stylisation section (pages 71-82), students create a themed environment for visitors to walk through. The environment consists of a series of still and moving images, sound collages, video presentations, interviews, etc illustrating aspects of the theme. Examples of themes might be:

- The evacuation experience
- The slave ship experience
- Charles Dickens' London
- The nuclear power plant experience

This is a more complex idea than other analogies and is most effective if the resources of a drama studio can be used. Students respond particularly well to the challenge if they are inviting their peers to attend.

Classroom management

Before
Have available various resources that help students to create their analogy (eg space for a studio set, a range of CDs, simple props, an OHP – very useful as a spotlight). Homework prior to the lesson could be to gather some of the resources they'll need.

During
Use the conventions of the analogy to retain order. Take on a role in the drama yourself, eg:
- The floor manager with cue boards (applause, silence) in a media show
- The high priest in a ritual
- The referee in a sports event or game

After
Have some form of reward where the context demands it. This could be a trophy, chocolate treats or an appropriate school award: house points, 'well done slips', etc.

So what's the benefit?

1 In terms of Bloom's Taxonomy (see pages 12-13) this technique encourages students to progress beyond Levels 1 and 2 of cognitive activity – knowledge and understanding – to Levels 3, 4 and 5 – application, analysis and synthesis. To create an analogy, students must understand what has been taught, restating and restructuring their understanding to fit the new form.

2 Students are keenly aware of contemporary media contexts, often far more so than their teachers. Most of them have been fed a diet of game shows, quizzes, soap operas and reality TV for their entire lives. They understand implicitly the conventions (working the audience through speed and tone of voice; repetition; the tense, hanging silence and the condescension of the presenter). They are confident and enthusiastic in using these conventions so the level of engagement in activities like this tends to be very high.

When should I use it?

Analogy is best suited to the end of a unit or scheme of work as it is summative in nature.

It takes	Objective information Theories Opinions Feelings Questions
Adds	+ A new context or form A different audience
And results in	= An original piece of presentation

Since they require lateral thinking and leaps of imagination, these techniques are useful for stretching more able students.

**Drama as
Active Learning**

 Drama Games

 Narrative

 Character

 Stylisation

 Analogies

 **Dilemmas and
Options** ◀

 Teacher in
Role and
Using Props

Dilemmas and
Options

What is it?

Decision-making is a key skill for students. Whether it's making an educational decision (eg which subject options to take at the transition from Key Stage 3 to Key Stage 4), a personal decision (eg about the use of contraception), or a decision within the context of a lesson (eg should capital punishment be restored?) students should be:

- Able to identify the options open to them and to grasp the differences, empathising with a range of points of view
- Informed about the consequences of their choice and tolerant of those who make a different choice
- Enabled to make a decision responsibly

These drama techniques offer ways to make options clear, to explore the consequences of different choices and to provide different structures within which students can demonstrate their personal decisions.

Technique 1: Spectrum

Indicate a real or imagined line across the working space. One end of the line represents one extreme of a decision (such as a clear *'Yes'*), the other end represents the opposite decision (a clear *'No'*). Positions on the line between the two extremes represent uncertainty but with a tendency to *'Yes'* or *'No'*.

The idea is to give students questions or statements to which they respond by standing at a point on the spectrum line. Students can see their opinion in relation to others'. For many, this helps clarify ideas which can then be more easily articulated.

Like this:  Abortion

Give the statement: *'Life begins at the moment of conception'*. Ask students to respond by taking a position on a spectrum line where one end signifies total agreement, the other total disagreement. A student who believes life begins in a very limited way at conception would stand at a position between 'No' and the centre.

Simple preference statements (eg *'I like bananas'*) can be used to make this technique work with even the youngest children.

Technique 2: Doorsteps

Six students stand as if behind doors on a street. They are given characters (eg, elderly deaf man, mother with crying baby, eco warrior, affluent young businesswoman, lonely 'single', couch potato). You go to each door and ask an opinion question such as: *'Why has Sir Alex Ferguson been such a successful football manager?'*. Students must respond in role, each attempting to give a different reason.

Like this: Using the example of Sir Alex

Student A: *'He had been a successful player before going into management.'*
Student B: *'He took over a successful club.'*
Student C: *'He was given a lot of money to spend on players...'* etc

This technique is useful for helping students to empathise with a range of viewpoints.

Technique 3: Conscience alley

Following a class discussion, students form two lines representing different options. All students devise a sentence/phrase to persuade a listener to choose their option. Students in turn walk down the alley while their classmates whisper their persuasive arguments. The effect is of weighing up the options before coming to a decision.

Conscience alley needs quite a large space but the effect on students can be dramatic. Hearing whispered voices is a far more intense experience than hearing loud voices or shouting.

Like this: Should an inhabited valley be flooded to build a reservoir?

Line 1 (in favour of the flooding):

'The population is decreasing'

'There is little agriculture'

'We need the water for the drought'

'Jobs will be created'

Line 2 (against the flooding):

'We've lived here for five generations'

'The next valley is totally uninhabited'

'A rare plant grows in the valley'

Technique 4: Forum theatre

Think of forum theatre in terms of a film sequence that can be rewound and altered to explore the consequences of different actions.

Take a moment of choice that a real or fictional character faces. Invite a small group of students to role-play the consequences of one choice. Halt the action when the consequences are clear. 'Rewind' and role-play (with the same or a different group) the consequences of a different choice. Repeat for as many choices as students can think of.

Like this: The arrest and crucifixion of Jesus
Start at the point of the betrayal and arrest of Jesus.
Role play 1 – Jesus gives a vocal defence of his innocence
Role play 2 – Jesus encourages the disciples to fight the arresting authorities
Role play 3 – Jesus performs a miracle and freezes the soldiers to the spot

This is a very effective technique for working through consequences. You'll find that students readily question unrealistic conclusions.

Classroom management

Before
It's helpful to have physical space to move about for many of these activities. The greater the space, the wider the range of options.

During
Give a clear countdown into decision-making time, indicating that all students should respond immediately. Be aware of students who attempt to avoid taking personal responsibility. A quiet word of encouragement may help.

After
Remind students that there is always the freedom to change their minds – as long as they have a good reason.

So what's the benefit?

These techniques offer a variety of ways to express options in non-verbal as well as verbal contexts, allowing for the fullest range of comprehension.

Also, for some students it takes courage to make a decision publicly, particularly if the decision has to be expressed in words. They fear ridicule, either because they might take the 'wrong' decision in terms of class democracy or because they are not able to verbalise the complexity of the dilemma in which they find themselves. These techniques enable decisions to be made and expressed without pressure and without high visibility. Some examples also try to tackle the counter issue of students who follow the 'acceptable' or majority decision of the crowd rather than engage with the issue for themselves.

Finally, the techniques encourage students to understand and tolerate a range of points of view, including those that contradict their own.

When should I use it?

You can use the techniques in this section:

- To illustrate the full range of options. Many of them allow students to collate the options. They are then able to observe, analyse, empathise and reflect

- When students are inhibited in taking clear personal decisions because of ability, age or personality. These techniques offer a variety of ways to respond

- When there is a range of possible responses. These may be difficult to express verbally but can be more easily expressed physically

Literature – ideas

❶ Forum theatre – stop the reading of a novel or play at a crucial stage in the plot. Students project what they think will happen next by acting it out. Rewind and allow other students to act out alternative outcomes.

❷ Spectrum – to distinguish between open and closed questions. Indicate an imaginary line across the room. Ask a series of questions. If the question is open then students stand at the yes end of the line, the no end if the question is closed. If the question is open to a variety of responses, students stand at a position on the line that indicates their opinion.

❸ Conscience alley – students form two lines that represent different options open to a character in a play or novel.

Music, art and design – ideas

1 Doorsteps – six students stand as if behind doors on a street. Give each student a character, ensuring a range of contrasting points of view. You go to each door in turn, show a copy of a famous work of art and ask for the students' opinions. Students must reply in role.

2 Spectrum – students represent instruments. The line represents prominence in a piece of music. Students move up and down the line as the music is played, indicating the prominence of their instrument.

Science and maths – ideas

1 Spectrum – use the spectrum line for responses to true/false revision questions based on previous learning.

2 Spectrum – draw two lines on the floor, marking them 0 to 9. One represents 10s, the other units. Students work in pairs. You give a mathematical problem, the answer to which is 99 or less. Students give the answer by standing on the appropriate combination of points on the spectrum. This can be increased to use 100s and 1000s by the use of additional lines.

3 Spectrum debate – two students stand at opposite ends of the spectrum line, representing opposing opinions (eg on stem cell research). Class stand at mid-point. Students alternately state arguments for and against. At the end of each statement class members are asked to indicate their point of agreement on the spectrum. They may move or stay still as they decide.

Modern foreign languages – ideas

1 Spectrum – use the spectrum line for responses to true/false revision questions on vocabulary.

2 Conscience alley – take a simple life choice (strawberries or oranges? Football or tennis?). Review the appropriate vocabulary and give students time to rehearse the arguments for one or the other. Walk the alley and be persuaded.

3 Doorsteps – review the vocabulary needed to express an opinion on a controversial subject. In a circle students stand behind the doors. You conduct a simple vox pop, moving swiftly from student to student.

PE and sport – ideas

❶ Spectrum – the line represents performance from 1 (poor) to 10 (excellent). As a self-assessment task students go and stand on the line. Peer assessment of the same student may indicate a different level of performance.

❷ Forum theatre – stop a game at certain points and discuss the optional moves open to a player (ball to feet, never stand still, short passes only, use the width of the pitch, etc). Rehearse the moves and discuss effect.

❸ Conscience alley – to discuss and raise awareness of the issues of confidence and frame of mind, create a conscience alley with whispered comments to raise and deflate confidence.

Social sciences – ideas

① Doorsteps – a valley is to be flooded to build a dam. You as planning officer interview students as residents of the valley. This can be done with students in a circle, taking random contributions.

② Forum theatre – students improvise a scene of family dysfunction (eg, an underage daughter reveals she's pregnant, a child steals money from a parent, a hung-over parent sleeps in and causes a child to be late for school). Discuss with students ways in which the situation might have been handled differently. Improvise the options, discussing outcomes.

③ Conscience alley – create a conscience alley for a person deciding whether to stay in a rural location or move to the city. Review the pros and cons before forming the alley.

Humanities – ideas

❶ Spectrum – use the spectrum line for responses to true/false revision of previous learning.

❷ Spectrum – use the spectrum line for students to indicate strength of opinion within the class (eg the age of sexual consent should be lowered to 14 – do you agree or disagree?). Students can discuss opinions with those at the same or different points on the line.

❸ Forum theatre – improvise an important historical turning point (eg within a battle). Stop the action, discuss the options and enact them, reviewing the consequences.

**Drama as
Active Learning**

Drama Games

Narrative

Character

Stylisation

Analogies

**Dilemmas and
Options**

**Teacher in
Role and
Using Props**

Teacher in Role
and Using Props

What is it?

Drama, essentially, is about assuming a role. This may require no more than to adopt a voice, place a hat on your head or wield an imaginary piece of equipment. We do it when reading a bedtime story to a child, joining in Christmas party games or recounting an amusing event to friends. When you assume a role in the classroom, however simple, you create opportunities for students to learn as they join you in role. Often their contributions will encourage and stimulate you in yours. Here's an example:

- You wish to give details about conditions in a Victorian workhouse
- You assume the role of the workhouse taskmaster. You rouse students from their slumbers with the promise of watery porridge and a crack (with a metre rule) if they don't get themselves moving, then set them their dirty and tedious tasks

When you assume roles, you step outside the limitations and expectations of period 4 on a Tuesday afternoon. You begin to **create an event** that has never happened before, not for the students and not for you. Together you enter new learning territory.

So what's the benefit?

When you use these techniques, factual information:

- Gains an **emotional impact** – students experience the Victorian orphans' life
- Is seen from more than one **perspective** – the taskmaster/the orphans
- Stimulates **questions** – why is the taskmaster brutal? Why don't the orphans rebel? Why were there so many orphans? Who organised the system?
- Leads to a student response – they feel **safer** in their assumed roles to challenge, suggest and question within the drama
- Gives a sense of **shared exploration** between yourself and the students

You can use them at the **start of a series of lessons** to introduce a new topic, to review previous learning or to spotlight and motivate particular students. They are also useful for giving **mid-lesson variety**, engaging students in a narrative, or demonstrating specific features or characteristics of raw materials, for example. At the **end of a unit of work** 'teacher in role' can be used to summarise learning that has taken place and to highlight achievement.

Classroom management

Before

- It's helpful to have a **simple item of costume or a prop** that defines the role. It needn't be elaborate (a hat, stick, coat or mug will offer many opportunities)

- Some moderate **rearrangement of the classroom** space may be beneficial (a circle/an open space/rows/clusters of tables)

- Rewrite lesson notes as **prompt cards**. Much of your role will be improvised

- A selection of **versatile objects** (metre rule/bucket/balloon/biscuit box, etc) always available in a corner of the room will allow for improvisation as you grow in confidence

Classroom management

During

- In my experience, students quickly grasp the shared rules of learning in role. They assume their own roles and respond in context. It's therefore important not to break the convention, eg by slipping into teacher mode for control techniques. You can play only one role at a time! So instead of *'Pay attention please, John,'* draw students back on task with comments appropriate to your role, eg (workhouse master) *'You boy! Keep silent or you'll catch a crack of this rod.'*

- Think about the status of your character within the drama:
  - high status – in control of events, giving orders
  - equal status – suggesting, discussing, giving warnings
  - low status – seeking help or advice

After

- Bring the role play to an end clearly, eg *'5, 4, 3, 2, 1... I'm now Mr/Mrs/Miss/Ms...'*

Literature – ideas

1 *Macbeth* – you are the cook commenting at the end of Act 1, Scene 6 on the banquet to welcome King Duncan. Invite other servants to make their comments.

2 You are the convenor of a committee deciding the top five poets/playwrights/novelists/children's books/poems, etc of all time. Students act as advocates for various writers or works.

3 *Goodnight Mr Tom* (or similar) – students in family groups receive an evacuation procedures letter. As evacuation officer you hold a public meeting.

4 As a Police Officer you announce that a woman has been found wandering the school in a confused state. All she can remember is her name (a central character from the current class reader). She has a handbag (produce prop). Students approach bag and pretend to extract items that explain her history and character.

Music, art and design – ideas

Use teacher in role to set a design brief. This provides students with a recognisable context (media, fashion, commerce) outside the classroom in which to place the task.

1 You are a radio station boss wishing to produce a series, *'Classic Music of the 20th Century'*. Ask the students to nominate 12 tracks, justifying their reasons.

2 You are a millionaire commissioning a piece of art. You give specific details of the style and medium. There are rumours of a huge fee!

3 You are the managing director of a cosmetics company launching a new perfume. You approach your top designers for a packaging design.

4 You are Dr. Doolittle getting tools in the workshop to describe their uses. Props encourage the sense of touch, particularly engaging kinaesthetic learners.

Science and maths – ideas

❶ You are a worm wriggling through the compost heap, meeting other creatures. Students use previous learning to adopt roles as these creatures.

❷ You are an absent-minded professor (use this character often!) who needs reminding about health and safety issues, methods, etc.

❸ You are Dr. Who, taking students on a time travel tour of the history of Maths. They must keep a diary of discoveries.

❹ Take on the role of a TV celebrity (Bill Oddie, David Bellamy, David Attenborough, though it needn't be a naturalist) to describe animal behaviour.

❺ Conduct a mental maths test in the style of a TV quiz with you as the compere.

Students engage with what might otherwise be mundane elements of a lesson.

Modern foreign languages – ideas

Teacher in role is already a common technique in MFL where creating 'real-life' contexts for using language is essential. As with any regularly-used routine, it's easy to lose the impact. Here are some ideas that develop the creative opportunities. You can adapt them for any language:

1 The owner of a hotel welcomes a coach party of tourists and gives them a tour of the facilities, eliciting responses to inadequate provision.

2 A Police Officer interviews witnesses to a crime.

3 A TV journalist interviews members of a victorious Olympic sports team.

4 Their plane is to be delayed by 24 hours and you, the airline representative, meet with the angry passengers.

PE and sport – ideas

❶ To start a lesson you are the PA announcer giving a run down on team members – you can use this to motivate less able students by appropriate exaggeration!

❷ An orienteering activity becomes a spy chase with clues to be discovered. You are the Spymaster. Less sports-minded students may more readily commit to an adventure scenario.

❸ To end a lesson you are a sports pundit commenting on team performance, picking out skills demonstrated. As well as providing engaging feedback, students can be interviewed and therefore take part in self-evaluation.

❹ You award sporting 'Oscars' for achievement – the focus can be directed on to the most improved performers with nominations by students themselves (an opportunity for peer evaluation).

Social sciences – ideas

1 A multi-national company wants to dam a river/chop down a forest/build a refinery. You are the convenor of the planning meeting. Students (following research) are experts from various interest groups.

2 A time capsule is to be buried (provide prop). Students approach the capsule and place an imaginary object in it, explaining how it represents this time, this place and these people – a summative activity following work on a social grouping.

3 You are an anthropologist leading a group of aid workers around a native community. Students in role ask questions about their surroundings.

4 Provide students with an Ordnance Survey map. You are a general attacking a named location on the map. Use topography and other features to plan your attack. (A peaceful option is to plan a large public event such as a music festival.)

Humanities – ideas

1 You convene a community meeting about the issue of religious tension. Students are representatives from various religious groups. You may wish to take a strong role, eg a fundamentalist Christian or Muslim.

2 You are a TV journalist conducting a vox pop on 'How can you tell that someone is British?'

3 You are a tour guide leading a group around a medieval monastery. Invite students in role to ask questions about their surroundings.

4 A box of found artefacts (real, if possible) is presented to the students. They are archaeologists who try to identify the function of each item.

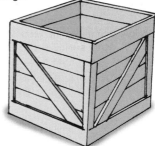

Take a bow

My favourite Oscars are those for Best Supporting Actor and Actress. They're not like silver medals, given to those who didn't quite make it. They're awarded for using drama skills in a particular way. These actors and actresses have supported, in other words **created the environment** in which the stars could excel.

You don't need to be a great actor to use drama techniques in teaching. You need simply to have the desire to create an environment in which students can excel. Yes, it requires a measure of confidence, but that grows with enthusiastic application. There'll be some nervousness and a little hesitation, but that will merely help you show empathy with your students in their learning.

If you've reached this point in the book you've probably been dipping in and out. Maybe you've used some of the techniques. That's the way to use it. Start where you feel comfortable and occasionally be a little more adventurous.

Open the wardrobe, take out a costume and away you go.

Books

Learning Through Imagined Experience
by Jonothan Neelands.
Published by Hodder and Stoughton

Structuring Drama Work
By Jonothan Neelands and Tony Goode
Published by Cambridge University Press

Using Drama in RE – Making the Abstract Concrete
By Brian Radcliffe
Published by The Stapleford Centre

WEBSITES
There are many good websites available with instructions for drama games. It's a question of pick and mix. Type 'drama games' into www.google.co.uk and see what takes your fancy.

About the author

Brian Radcliffe

Brian Radcliffe is a teacher and freelance writer with over 30 years' experience in teaching, training and lecturing from pre-school to adult education. Trained originally as a secondary level English and Drama teacher, Brian spent 15 years as Minister of a Baptist church in the north of England, using drama extensively within the liturgy and outreach of the church. Returning to secondary education, he has specialised in implementing the use of drama as a teaching resource across the curriculum.

Brian has written extensively for the educational market, particularly within the fields of citizenship, drama workshops and assembly scripts. He is strongly committed to promoting learning that is active in style and begins where students are.

He is available to help develop ideas contained in this book and can be contacted at bandsrad@hotmail.com (please title your email Drama for Learning).

Order Form

Your details

Name _____

Position _____

School _____

Address _____

_____

Telephone _____

Fax _____

E-mail _____

VAT No. (EC only) _____

Your Order Ref _____

Please send me:

No. copies

Drama for Learning _____ Pocketbook ☐

_____ Pocketbook ☐

_____ Pocketbook ☐

_____ Pocketbook ☐

_____ Pocketbook ☐

Order by Post

Teachers' Pocketbooks

Laurel House, Station Approach
Alresford, Hants. SO24 9JH UK

Order by Phone, Fax or Internet

Telephone: +44 (0)1962 735573
Facsimile: +44 (0)1962 733637
E-mail: sales@teacherspocketbooks.co.uk
Web: www.teacherspocketbooks.co.uk